LIFE JOURNAL

My Story Journal

Date:____________________ Time:_______________

Things I Want to Do

What Am I Feeling Today

Things Im ReallyPicky About

Wish List

Regrets

My Story Journal

Date:____________________ Time:_______________

Things I Want to Do

What Am I Feeling Today

Things Im ReallyPicky About

Wish List

Regrets

My Story Journal

Date:____________________ Time:______________

Things I Want to Do

____

____

____

____

____

____

____

____

What Am I Feeling Today

Things Im ReallyPicky About

Wish List

Regrets

My Story Journal

Date:____________________ Time:______________

Things I Want to Do

What Am I Feeling Today

Things Im ReallyPicky About

Wish List

Regrets

My Story Journal

Date:____________________ Time:_______________

Things I Want to Do

What Am I Feeling Today

Things Im ReallyPicky About

Wish List

Regrets

My Story Journal

Date:____________________ Time:______________

Things I Want to Do

What Am I Feeling Today

Things Im ReallyPicky About

Wish List

Regrets

My Story Journal

Date:___________________ Time:______________

Things I Want to Do

What Am I Feeling Today	Things Im ReallyPicky About

Wish List	Regrets

My Story Journal

Date:____________________ Time:______________

Things I Want to Do

What Am I Feeling Today

Things Im ReallyPicky About

Wish List

Regrets

My Story Journal

Date:____________________ Time:_______________

Things I Want to Do

What Am I Feeling Today

Things Im ReallyPicky About

Wish List

Regrets

My Story Journal

Date:______________________ Time:________________

Things I Want to Do

What Am I Feeling Today

Things Im ReallyPicky About

Wish List

Regrets

My Story Journal

Date:____________________ Time:______________

Things I Want to Do

____

____

____

____

____

____

____

____

What Am I Feeling Today

Things Im Really Picky About

Wish List

Regrets

My Story Journal

Date:____________________ Time:______________

Things I Want to Do

What Am I Feeling Today

Things Im Really Picky About

Wish List

Regrets

My Story Journal

Date:____________________ Time:______________

Things I Want to Do

What Am I Feeling Today	Things Im ReallyPicky About

Wish List	Regrets

My Story Journal

Date:____________________ Time:_______________

Things I Want to Do

What Am I Feeling Today

Things Im ReallyPicky About

Wish List

Regrets

My Story Journal

Date:____________________ Time:_______________

Things I Want to Do

What Am I Feeling Today

Things Im Really Picky About

Wish List

Regrets

My Story Journal

Date:____________________ Time:______________

Things I Want to Do

What Am I Feeling Today

Things Im ReallyPicky About

Wish List

Regrets

My Story Journal

Date:____________________ Time:________________

Things I Want to Do

What Am I Feeling Today

Things Im ReallyPicky About

Wish List

Regrets

My Story Journal

Date:__________________ Time:______________

Things I Want to Do

What Am I Feeling Today

Things Im ReallyPicky About

Wish List

Regrets

My Story Journal

Date:____________________ Time:_______________

Things I Want to Do

What Am I Feeling Today

Things Im Really Picky About

Wish List

Regrets

My Story Journal

Date:____________________ Time:_______________

Things I Want to Do

What Am I Feeling Today

Things Im ReallyPicky About

Wish List

Regrets

My Story Journal

Date:____________________ Time:_______________

Things I Want to Do

What Am I Feeling Today

Things Im ReallyPicky About

Wish List

Regrets

My Story Journal

Date:____________________ Time:______________

Things I Want to Do

What Am I Feeling Today

Things Im ReallyPicky About

Wish List

Regrets

My Story Journal

Date:____________________ Time:______________

Things I Want to Do

What Am I Feeling Today

Things Im ReallyPicky About

Wish List

Regrets

My Story Journal

Date:____________________ Time:______________

Things I Want to Do

What Am I Feeling Today

Things Im ReallyPicky About

Wish List

Regrets

My Story Journal

Date:____________________ Time:_______________

Things I Want to Do

What Am I Feeling Today

Things Im Really Picky About

Wish List

Regrets

My Story Journal

Date:____________________ Time:______________

Things I Want to Do

What Am I Feeling Today

Things Im ReallyPicky About

Wish List

Regrets

My Story Journal

Date:______________________ Time:_______________

Things I Want to Do

What Am I Feeling Today	Things Im ReallyPicky About

Wish List	Regrets

My Story Journal

Date:____________________ Time:______________

Things I Want to Do

____

____

____

____

____

____

____

____

What Am I Feeling Today

Things Im ReallyPicky About

Wish List

Regrets

My Story Journal

Date:____________________ Time:______________

Things I Want to Do

What Am I Feeling Today

Things Im Really Picky About

Wish List

Regrets

My Story Journal

Date:____________________ Time:______________

Things I Want to Do

What Am I Feeling Today

Things Im Really Picky About

Wish List

Regrets

My Story Journal

Date:______________________ Time:________________

Things I Want to Do

What Am I Feeling Today

Things Im ReallyPicky About

Wish List

Regrets

My Story Journal

Date:____________________ Time:______________

Things I Want to Do

What Am I Feeling Today

Things Im ReallyPicky About

Wish List

Regrets

My Story Journal

Date:____________________ Time:______________

Things I Want to Do

____
____
____
____
____
____
____
____

What Am I Feeling Today

Things Im Really Picky About

Wish List

Regrets

My Story Journal

Date:____________________ Time:_______________

Things I Want to Do

What Am I Feeling Today

Things Im ReallyPicky About

Wish List

Regrets

My Story Journal

Date:____________________ Time:______________

Things I Want to Do

What Am I Feeling Today

Things Im ReallyPicky About

Wish List

Regrets

My Story Journal

Date:____________________ Time:______________

Things I Want to Do

What Am I Feeling Today

Things Im ReallyPicky About

Wish List

Regrets

My Story Journal

Date:____________________ Time:_______________

Things I Want to Do

What Am I Feeling Today

Things Im ReallyPicky About

Wish List

Regrets

My Story Journal

Date:____________________ Time:_______________

Things I Want to Do

What Am I Feeling Today

Things Im Really Picky About

Wish List

Regrets

My Story Journal

Date:____________________ Time:______________

Things I Want to Do

What Am I Feeling Today	Things Im ReallyPicky About

Wish List	Regrets

My Story Journal

Date:____________________ Time:______________

Things I Want to Do

What Am I Feeling Today

Things Im ReallyPicky About

Wish List

Regrets

My Story Journal

Date:____________________ Time:_______________

Things I Want to Do

What Am I Feeling Today

Things Im ReallyPicky About

Wish List

Regrets

My Story Journal

Date:______________________ Time:______________

Things I Want to Do

What Am I Feeling Today

Things Im ReallyPicky About

Wish List

Regrets

My Story Journal

Date:____________________ Time:______________

Things I Want to Do

What Am I Feeling Today

Things Im ReallyPicky About

Wish List

Regrets

My Story Journal

Date:____________________ Time:_______________

Things I Want to Do

What Am I Feeling Today

Things Im ReallyPicky About

Wish List

Regrets

My Story Journal

Date:____________________ Time:______________

Things I Want to Do

What Am I Feeling Today

Things Im Really Picky About

Wish List

Regrets

My Story Journal

Date:____________________ Time:______________

Things I Want to Do

What Am I Feeling Today

Things Im ReallyPicky About

Wish List

Regrets

My Story Journal

Date:____________________ Time:_______________

Things I Want to Do

What Am I Feeling Today

Things Im Really Picky About

Wish List

Regrets

My Story Journal

Date:____________________ Time:______________

Things I Want to Do

What Am I Feeling Today

Things Im ReallyPicky About

Wish List

Regrets

www.ingramcontent.com/pod-product-compliance
Lightning Source LLC
LaVergne TN
LVHW082301150826
845677LV00009B/1682